What Do You Know About
Earth's Atmosphere?

PowerKiDS
press
New York

Gillian Gosman

Published in 2014 by The Rosen Publishing Group, Inc.
29 East 21st Street, New York, NY 10010

First Edition

Editor: Jennifer Way
Book Design: Kate Laczynski
Layout Design: Andrew Povolny

Photo Credits: Cover Planetobserver/Science Photo Library/Getty Images; p. 5 2happy/Shutterstock.com; p. 6 Hemera/Thinkstock; p. 7 Encyclopaedia Britannica/Universal Images Group/Getty Images; p. 8 Stockbyte/Thinkstock; p. 9 First Class Photos/Shutterstock.com; p. 10 Martin Harvey/Peter Arnold/Getty Images; p. 11 Claudio Sepúlveda Geoffroy/Flickr/Getty Images; pp. 13–14 Dave Brosha Photography/Flickr/Getty Images; pp. 14, 21, 22 iStockphoto/Thinkstock; p. 15 Photo Researchers Inc/Getty Images; p. 17 djgis/Shutterstock.com; p. 18 Harry Kikstra/Flickr/Getty Images; p. 19 Leonard Lessin/Photo Researchers/Getty Images; p. 20 Marco Brivio/Photographer's Choice RF.

Gosman, Gillian.
 What do you know about earth's atmosphere? / by Gillian Gosman. — 1st ed.
    p. cm. — (20 questions: Earth science)
 Includes index.
 ISBN 978-1-4488-9699-8 (library binding) — ISBN 978-1-4488-9856-5 (pbk.) — ISBN 978-1-4488-9857-2 (6-pack)
 1. Atmosphere—Juvenile literature. 2. Weather—Juvenile literature. 3. Air pressure—Juvenile literature. 4. Temperature—Juvenile literature. I. Title.
 QC863.5.G67 2013
 551.5—dc23
                                        2012030676

Manufactured in the United States of America

CPSIA Compliance Information: Batch #S13PK5: For Further Information contact Rosen Publishing, New York, New York at 1-800-237-9932

Contents

What Do You Know About Earth's Atmosphere?

Earth's atmosphere is pretty special. To see just how special, let's take a look at the atmosphere of the planet Mars. Mars's atmosphere is thin and is made almost entirely of a gas called carbon dioxide.

If Earth's atmosphere were replaced by Mars's atmosphere, life as we know it would end. Unable to breathe the carbon dioxide in the air, all living things would die. The planet would overheat. The oceans would dry up and disappear.

What is it about Earth's atmosphere that makes life on Earth possible? In this book, we will explore what Earth's atmosphere is and how it works.

Earth's atmosphere changes with altitude, or distance from the ground. You will learn why later in this book.

1. What is the atmosphere?

Earth's atmosphere is a layer of air surrounding our planet. Air is all around us. We cannot see it or touch it, but all life on Earth depends on it. Air is made up of several kinds of gas. Depending on where you are, the air might also contain tiny pieces of other materials.

In this photo you can see where the edge of Earth's atmosphere blends with space.

Earth's Atmosphere

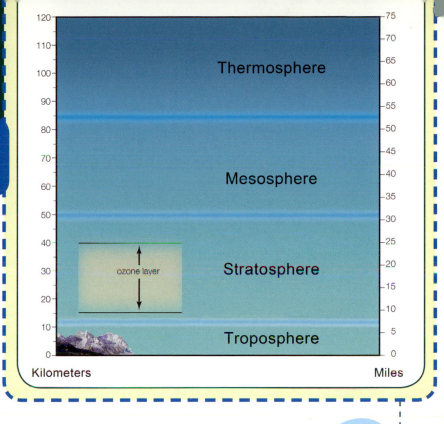

This diagram shows the layers of Earth's atmosphere from the ground to the thermosphere. The thermosphere continues about 150 miles (241 km) above what is shown here, where it blends into space.

2. What are the layers of the atmosphere called?

Earth's atmosphere is divided into layers. The layer closest to the ground is called the **troposphere**. About 7 miles (11 km) above Earth's surface, the troposphere ends and the **stratosphere** begins. Above the stratosphere is the **mesosphere**, followed by the **thermosphere**.

3. What is Earth's atmosphere made of?

Earth's atmosphere is made up of about 78 percent nitrogen, 21 percent oxygen, and 1 percent other gases. In most parts of the world, there is also water vapor in the atmosphere.

Earth's atmosphere is the densest within 10 miles (16 km) of the ground. A space shuttle needs a lot of power to push through the atmosphere to reach space.

4. How thick is Earth's atmosphere?

Earth's atmosphere is about 300 miles (480 km) thick. The air is denser, or thicker with gases, water, and other materials, closer to Earth's surface. As one moves away from Earth's surface, the air becomes thinner. The atmosphere does not end at a certain altitude. Rather, it fades into space.

Ozone is a gas in our atmosphere. There is a layer of ozone in the stratosphere. The **ozone layer** plays a very important role in the lives of all living things on Earth. It blocks some of the Sun's powerful and dangerous rays.

Earth's atmosphere protects us from the full power of the Sun's rays. Too much sunlight can still be harmful, though.

6. Where does weather form?

Weather forms in the troposphere. The troposphere is the most changeable layer of the atmosphere because this is where the effects of land, air, and water meet and create weather.

Airplanes fly high up in the troposphere, usually above where clouds form.

In the troposphere, the temperature drops as the altitude gets higher. As water vapor rises in the troposphere, it cools and **condenses**, forming clouds. Water vapor also condenses around particles in the air, grows heavy, and falls to the ground as precipitation. Precipitation includes rain, snow, sleet, and hail.

Areas of warm and cold air move around the planet, along with these clouds. This air is affected by the Sun as well as the land and water it passes over. It may become warmer, cooler, drier, or more humid. These changes all create different kinds of weather.

The type of precipitation that falls depends on the temperature. If the temperature is above 32° F (0° C), as it is in this picture, the precipitation that falls will likely be rain.

An **aurora** is a pattern of light in the night sky over the far northern and far southern regions of Earth. In the north it is called the aurora borealis, in the south it is called the aurora australis. The light may be green, pink, yellow, blue, or violet. It appears to "dance" or ripple across the sky.

Auroras are caused by **solar wind**. The solar wind carries charged particles from the Sun. These particles collide with, or crash into, Earth's **magnetic field**. Earth's magnetic field is weaker near the poles, so some of these particles pass through it. When this happens, the particles collide with the gases in Earth's thermosphere, causing the aurora.

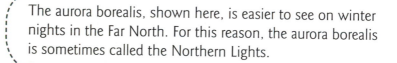

The aurora borealis, shown here, is easier to see on winter nights in the Far North. For this reason, the aurora borealis is sometimes called the Northern Lights.

9. How does Earth's atmosphere protect the planet?

The Sun gives off heat and **ultraviolet rays**. Living things need each of these things in small amounts, but too much of them can be deadly. Earth's atmosphere keeps the planet warm, yet protects it from the full power of the Sun's rays.

10. What is solar radiation?

The Sun gives off energy in the form light and heat. This energy is solar radiation.

The gases that absorb the Sun's radiation are called greenhouse gases. That is because they act a lot like a greenhouse, which lets in sunlight and traps heat inside.

11. How much of the Sun's radiation is absorbed or reflected?

The atmosphere absorbs, or holds in, some of the heat of the Sun. It reflects, or sends back out, the rest. About 70 percent of the Sun's radiation is absorbed by Earth's atmosphere and its surface. The other 30 percent is reflected back into space.

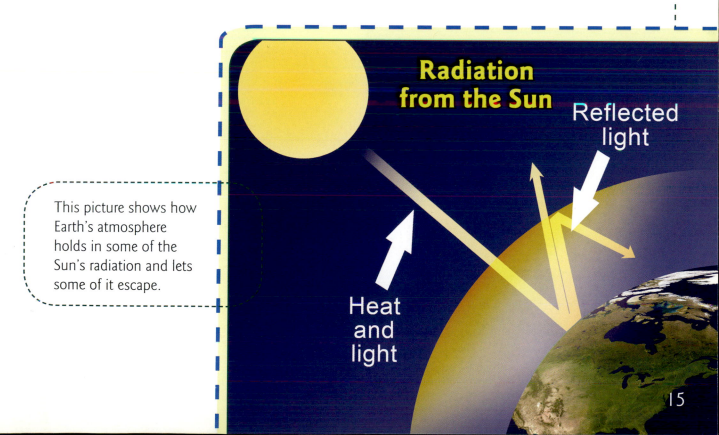

This picture shows how Earth's atmosphere holds in some of the Sun's radiation and lets some of it escape.

Radiation from the Sun

Reflected light

Heat and light

15

Radiant energy travels in waves. The **electromagnetic spectrum** is a scale of the wavelengths of different types of radiant energy. At one end of the spectrum are radio waves, which have long wavelengths. At the other end are gamma rays, which have short wavelengths. In the middle of the spectrum is visible light, or light that we can see.

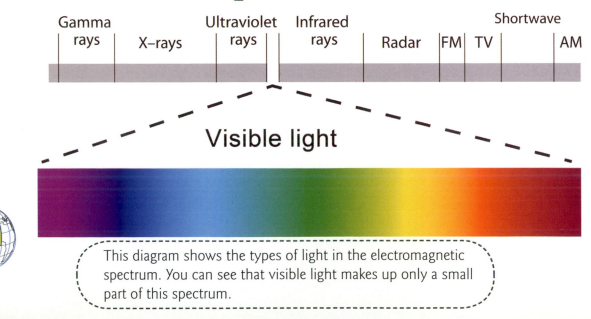

Gamma rays | X–rays | Ultraviolet rays | Infrared rays | Radar | FM | TV | Shortwave | AM

Visible light

This diagram shows the types of light in the electromagnetic spectrum. You can see that visible light makes up only a small part of this spectrum.

13. Why does the sky look blue?

Sunlight is a combination of colors, each with a slightly different wavelength. When sunlight enters the atmosphere, its rays collide with gases and particles of dust. Shorter-wavelength light, such as red light, is more easily absorbed by the gas and dust, while longer-wavelength light, such as blue light, is reflected in every direction. This makes the sky look blue.

Blue Sky

14. What is air pressure?

Air pressure is the weight of the air. Air pressure is measured using a barometer.

At the top of Mount Everest, the low air pressure makes the air "thin" and people need tanks of air to breathe.

15. Why does air pressure change with altitude?

Air pressure changes with changes in altitude. At **sea level**, the full mass of Earth's atmosphere presses down on you. At the top of a mountain, the air pressure is lower because less of the mass of Earth's atmosphere is pressing down on you.

Barometer

16. Why does the temperature change with altitude?

The air on a mountaintop is farther away from Earth's warm surface, so the temperature goes down as your altitude increases. The temperature increases in the stratosphere. That is because the ozone layer is absorbing the Sun's heat and light. The temperature drops again in the mesosphere. The temperature rises again in the thermosphere because the air there absorbs a lot of the Sun's heat.

17. What particulates are found in the air?

Earth's atmosphere contains many different particulates, or particles. These include dust, volcanic ash, pollen, ocean salt, and spores. Humans also add particulate matter to the atmosphere through air pollution.

18. How do particulates cause air pollution?

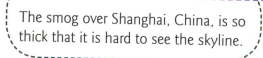

The smog over Shanghai, China, is so thick that it is hard to see the skyline.

Particulates can attach to other particulates and form **smog**. Water vapor can condense around particulates to create **acid rain**. Scientists measure the amount of particulate matter in the air to determine if the air is unhealthy to breathe.

19. How does carbon dioxide affect Earth's atmosphere?

Carbon dioxide is a greenhouse gas. Greenhouse gases help hold in the planet's heat. Cars, planes, factories, and anything else that runs on **fossil fuels** add extra carbon dioxide to the atmosphere. Scientists believe the increase in greenhouse gases is causing climate change. Climate change can cause polar ice to melt and cause other destructive weather patterns.

Flowers release pollen into the air.

20. What can be done to protect Earth's atmosphere?

There are small steps we can take to protect the atmosphere. We can use less fossil fuel by carpooling, riding a bike, or walking to our destinations. The less energy you use, the less pollution is created in making that energy. You can save energy by doing things like turning off lights or unplugging electronics.

You can also reuse and recycle many things. This keeps trash out of landfills, and it cuts down on the need to make brand-new items. These are all things you can do every day to help make Earth's atmosphere a little healthier.

One thing changes in Earth's atmosphere have done is lead to more serious droughts, or dry periods, in some places.

Glossary

acid rain (A-sud RAYN) Rainwater that is polluted by chemicals in the air.

aurora (uh-RAWR-uh) A band of often colorful light that sometimes occurs in the night sky in far northern and southern parts of the world.

condenses (kun-DENTS-ez) Cools and changes from a gas to a liquid.

electromagnetic spectrum (ih-lek-troh-mag-NEH-tik SPEK-trum) All the frequencies in which light waves, radio waves, and other waves can be found.

fossil fuels (FO-sul FYOOLZ) Fuels, such as coal, natural gas, or gasoline, that were made from plants that died millions of years ago.

magnetic field (mag-NEH-tik FEELD) A strong force made by currents that flow through metals and other matter.

mesosphere (MEH-zuh-sfir) The layer of the atmosphere between the stratosphere and the thermosphere.

ozone layer (OH-zohn LAY-er) A part of Earth's atmosphere.

sea level (SEE LEH-vul) The height of the top of the ocean.

smog (SMOG) Pollution in the air.

solar wind (SOH-ler WIND) Tiny pieces of charged matter that flow from the Sun.

stratosphere (STRA-tuh-sfir) The second layer of Earth's atmosphere as you move away from Earth.

thermosphere (THER-muh-sfir) The fourth layer of Earth's atmosphere.

troposphere (TROH-puh-sfeer) The layer of air that is closest to Earth's surface.

ultraviolet rays (ul-truh-VY-uh-let RAYZ) Rays given off by the Sun that can hurt your skin and eyes.

Index

Websites

Due to the changing nature of Internet links, PowerKids Press has developed an online list of websites related to the subject of this book. This site is updated regularly. Please use this link to access the list:
www.powerkidslinks.com/20es/atmos/